123
SESAME STREET®

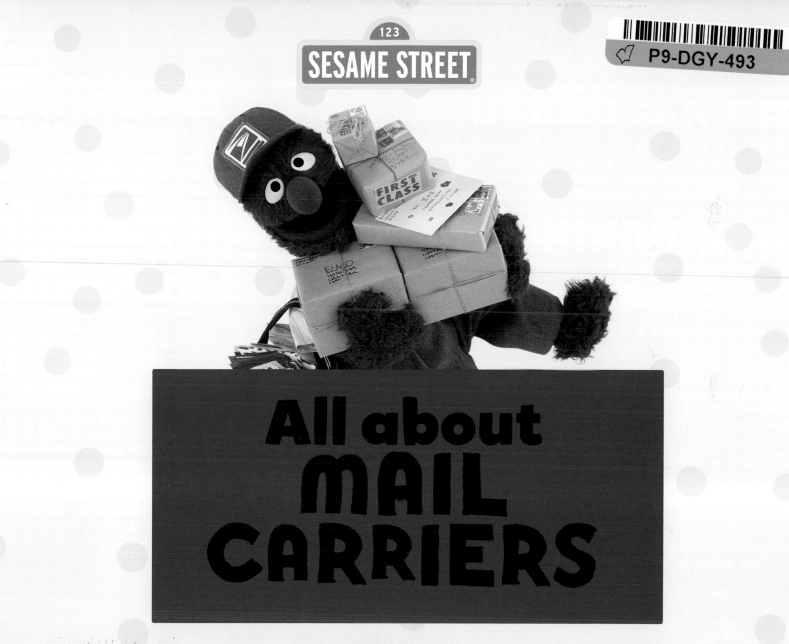

All about MAIL CARRIERS

Mari Schuh

Lerner Publications ◆ Minneapolis

Who are the people in your neighborhood?

Sesame Street has always been set smack in the middle of a friendly, busy community. We know that for all children, getting to know their communities is crucially important. So is understanding that everyone in the neighborhood—including kids!—has a part to play. In the *Sesame Street® Loves Community Helpers* books, *Sesame Street*'s favorite furry friends help young readers get to know some of these helpers better.

Sincerely,
The Editors at
Sesame Workshop

Table of Contents

Mail Carriers Are Amazing!

Hi, Mr. Mail Carrier! Elmo loves mail!

ELMO

Staying in Touch

Mail carriers are busy community helpers. They deliver everyone's mail.

We send letters to our friends.

Mail carriers wear uniforms.

They wear special shirts and pants. Some also wear coats and hats.

Mail carriers collect all the mail that is sent.

They collect mail at post offices, mailboxes, and drop-off bins.

Some mail carriers work in post offices. Others deliver the mail.

I'd like to buy the guitar stamps. ¡Gracias!

At the post office, they sell stamps and weigh packages.

Mail carriers sort mail.

Me like kind of mail that comes with cookies! Cowabunga!

Mail goes all around the world. Is that not awesome?

The mail is sorted and ready to go.

Mail carriers deliver mail everywhere, from cities to the country.

Some mail carriers drive mail trucks.

Mail trucks have eagles on them. Eagles are birds—like Big Bird!

Others walk and carry mail in big bags. Some push carts of mail.

Each mail carrier has a route.

A package! It's my birdseed of the month club delivery.

Mail carriers deliver letters, magazines, and packages on their routes.

Mail carriers work hard.

Thank you, Mr. Mail Carrier!

You're welcome, Elmo!

They deliver mail every day but Sundays and holidays!

Mail carriers work on sunny, snowy, windy, and rainy days.

But in very bad weather, they stay safe at home.

Mail carriers help us stay in touch with the people we love.

They are great community helpers!

Wow, a letter from my friend who lives far away!

Thank You, Mail Carriers!

It's your turn. Write a thank-you note to your mail carrier.

Dear Mail Carrier,

Thanks for bringing Elmo mail. Elmo is always excited to get mail and see you!

Your friend,

Elmo

Picture Glossary

deliver: to bring something to someone

post offices: places where people buy stamps and send mail

route: places that a mail carrier regularly delivers mail to

uniforms: special sets of clothes that mail carriers wear

Read More

Donner, Erica. *Post Office.* Minneapolis: Jump!, 2017.

Kenan, Tessa. *Hooray for Mail Carriers!* Minneapolis: Lerner Publications, 2018.

Murray, Julie. *The Post Office.* Minneapolis: Abdo Kids, 2017.

Index

Photo Acknowledgments

Additional image credits: Obradovic/Getty Images, p. 5; PeopleImages/Getty Images, pp. 6, 9, 21, 24, 30; Tetra Images/Getty Images, p. 7; Paul Bradbury/Getty Images, pp. 8, 15, 26, 30; DougSchneiderPhoto/Getty Images, p. 10; imagean/Getty Images, p. 11; SDI Productions/Getty Images, pp. 12-13, 30; zoranm/Getty Images, p. 14; gk-6mt/Getty Images, p. 16; Cohen/Ostrow/ Getty Images, p. 17; Victor Maschek/Shutterstock.com, p. 18; Kim Steele/Getty Images, p. 19; monkeybusinessimages/Getty Images, pp. 20, 29-30; Westend61/Getty Images, p. 23; Boston Globe/ Getty Images, p. 25; andresr/Getty Images, p. 27.

Cover: PeopleImages/Getty Images.

For my husband, Joe, who understands that getting mail is a highlight of my day

Lerner Publications Company
An imprint of Lerner Publishing Group, Inc.
241 First Avenue North
Minneapolis, MN 55401 USA

For reading levels and more information, look up this title at www.lernerbooks.com.

Main body text set in Mikado Medium.
Typeface provided by HVD Fonts.

Editor: Rebecca Higgins **Photo Editor:** Rebecca Higgins
Lerner team: Martha Kranes

Library of Congress Cataloging-in-Publication Data

Names: Schuh, Mari C., 1975– author.
Title: All about mail carriers / Mari Schuh.
Description: Minneapolis : Lerner Publications, 2021. | Series: Sesame Street loves community helpers | Includes bibliographical references and Index. | Audience: Ages 4–8 | Audience: Grades K–I | Summary: "Elmo loves mail! Mail carriers help their communities by sending and delivering mail. Elmo and other lovable Muppets celebrate mail carriers"– Provided by publisher.
Identifiers: LCCN 2019041628 (print) | LCCN 2019041629 (ebook) | ISBN 9781541589995 (library binding) | ISBN 9781728400945 (ebook)
Subjects: LCSH: Letter carriers–Juvenile literature.
Classification: LCC HE6241 .S34 2020 (print) | LCC HE6241 (ebook) | DDC 383/.145–dc23

LC record available at https://lccn.loc.gov/2019041628
LC ebook record available at https://lccn.loc.gov/2019041629

Manufactured in the United States of America
1-47509-48053-12/27/2019